W9-CIK-713

SCHOLARSHIP
More Great Cartoons from the *Kappan*

Edited by Kristin Herzog and Mary P. Miller

Published by Phi Delta Kappa
P.O. Box 789, Bloomington, IN 47402

©1985 by Phi Delta Kappa

Library of Congress Catalog Card Number 85-063148

ISBN 0-87367-796-X

Cover illustration by Jim Hull

Book design by Kristin Herzog and Mary P. Miller

Foreword

Here we go again. In the great tradition of Hollywood, we've been forced to produce a sequel. Two years ago the *Kappan* staff sifted through every cartoon that we'd published in the past 13 years and published *Recess Time*. We had no idea how well it would sell — or even if it would sell at all.

Why did we embark on such a risky venture, then? I'm tempted to blame it all on Kristin Herzog, our design director. Hers was the idea of a book of cartoons. But when she first came up with the idea, I realized that she'd plugged into something significant. I realized how many *Kappan* readers had shamefacedly confessed to me their great affection for our cartoons. Our busy readers may not always find time to study each and every feature article, but they always make time to skim through every single cartoon.

Recess Time was a hit (obviously, else we wouldn't be coming out with a sequel). So Kris, our designer Mary Miller, Pauline Gough, Bruce Smith, and I looked back through the last hundred or so issues of the *Kappan* and came up with another batch of cartoons that we think is every bit as funny as the preceding collection. We borrowed the title, *Scholarship*, from the cover drawing by Jim Hull, who contributes the quirky drawings that illustrate the Research section in the *Kappan*.

We know that readers of the *Kappan* take their work seriously. But they don't have to take themselves too seriously. That's the kiss of death. We suggest, as an antidote, the kiss of humor.

Robert W. Cole, Jr.
Editor
Phi Delta Kappan

The Effects of Technology

"If school were as important as they say it is, we wouldn't have to go. It would be televised."

12/84

"Well, today we learned to reorder segments on a random-access videodisc through the process of microcomputer interfacing."

10/83

"We're getting a new computer in our class today. I hope I'm the one it replaces."

2/85

"Dot-matrix homework is not acceptable."

"I can accept and process data, but I have trouble generating it on my own."

"We're gradually kicking the television habit. Now we're watching it with the sound off."

11/83

"Join me in welcoming our new staff members. Mr. Simpson, art. Ms. Dawes, science. Mr. Silbert, computer repairman."

"I like educational toys. I like educational TV. I like educational reading material. It's education I don't like."

"Well, at least now we know how they did those complicated astronomical calculations!"

10/83

"But if you didn't have TV till you were 12, what did you look at?"

"This is a pretty good book. It could probably even be made into a three- or four-part miniseries."

"I made it through mainstreaming, busing, teacher burnout, and state and local cutbacks. Just when things looked brighter, along comes 'The Software Search.'"

12/83

"My mom's an Ed.D., my dad's an M.D./Ph.D., and I'm a CBS, ABC, NBC."

4/85

"We are experiencing technical difficulties. Go read a book."

6/79

"Mrs. Broderick isn't as user-friendly as our teaching machines."

4/84

"Sure it's sloppy! You ever try to do homework and watch TV at the same time?"

11/78

"Why haven't you turned it on, Mom? You know I like to come home to a warm TV."

5/84

Curriculum and Back to Basics

I learned a lot in the public schools

IN HISTORY I LEARNED PATRIOTISM

IN MATH I LEARNED EFFICIENT, IMPERSONAL ANALYSIS

In English I absorbed obfuscatory semantology

IN **SPORTS** I LEARNED TO HATE THE ENEMY

I LEARNED THAT COST-EFFECTIVENESS, CONFORMITY, AND THE STATUS-QUO ARE BASIC

ART, MUSIC, AND LANGUAGES ARE NOT BASIC

NOW I FIGURE I'M EITHER READY FOR COLLEGE...

...OR BASIC TRAINING.

"I realize it has no value, but I strongly believe in basic research."

12/83

"I'm going to skip a lot of basic stuff and go straight into teaching you how to shelter your incomes."

10/84

"AMELIORATE. A-M-E-L-I-O-R-A-T-E. AMELIORATE."

"His school seems to be emphasizing a classical education."

1/84

"I think I'm on to something. By just banging two stones together, I'm able to make lots of little stones."

10/84

"I thought love made the world go round."

1/84

"Jason, 'reemphasizing basic skills' is not the same as 'jamming a little math and spelling down their throats'!"

3/78

"My daddy built it."

4/85

"*I suppose you want an immediate answer.*"

"Miss Renfrew certainly has done wonders with her rhythm band — although, personally, I never cared much for Stravinsky. . ."

3/84

11/83

The Search
for Excellence

"What does 'self-explanatory' mean?"

"I don't care if he does have an I.Q. of 169 — I still think he's faking."

9/69

"In school, I took accelerated math, accelerated English, and accelerated science. Then, for some unexplainable reason, I slowed down and came to a sudden stop."

12/84

"No, Timmy, not 'I sawed *the chair*'. 'I saw *the chair*' *or* 'I have seen *the chair*'."

"Somehow, to me a two-year college just naturally sounds better than a four-year college."

11/84

"I see that what we have been calling 'on task' is now to be called 'engaged learning time.' What was it before? 'Getting down to work,' wasn't it?"

3/84

"Ignorance isn't bliss."

"Mr. Branson is a perpetual student."

"It's Freddy's parents. They want you to tell them again how gifted he is."

3/84

"Forty-three percent of those questioned didn't know the answers."

1/85

"Don't be angry with him. It's an educational *noisemaker."*

"Three D's and two F's. Hey, that's great! A full house."

"Math D, English F, History D — and I see a journey."

6/84

"Oh, it's a field trip for an advanced class in the mathematics of probability."

12/83

"Well, we've achieved political, academic, sexual, and personal freedom. The only thing left to do now, I guess, is take some courses."

"To put it mildly, Ms. Tibbs, your Jimmy has a terribly uncluttered mind."

"Momentum."

"I can't explain what I just read, because I wasn't listening."

"So we feel that, for a third-grader, Harold is quite advanced. That goes for his wife, too."

6/84

"If it's any consolation to you, I no longer think you're capable of doing better work."

11/83

"No, Billy, the difference between 10 and 6 is not a rather gray area."

2/85

"Well, next time you invoke the muses, don't mumble."

2/84

"I thought at first I was on to something, but it's only a phone number."

"If you want to see real results, get me a couple of corporate sponsors."

9/84

"No need to say anything, Dean Wilson. I can tell you're disappointed in me!"

4/85

Coping with Teaching

PROFESSOR
BLAIRD OGLESBY

PUBLISHED   1952
PERISHED   1979

SCHWADRON

"I'd like you to meet my substitute teacher."

4/85

"I'm afraid I've thoroughly messed up the seating chart, so you must take care to remember your new names."

3/84

"I'm giving you a 'Marginal' on your attitude toward constructive criticism."

1/85

10/84

"I know how tempting it is, Miss Tutwiler, but you really shouldn't dismiss your class for summer recess until summer gets here."

9/84

"You say you were a high school band instructor?"

"What did you bring to school today, Tommy?"

"Watch this! All I have to do to get Coach Cranston to change the subject to sports is to throw him this football!"

12/83

"The principal would like another look at your diploma."

3/85

"Number three is Mr. Hugo, our seventh-grade teacher — the one whose exam contained questions not covered in the assigned reading."

11/84

50

"It's very nice that you brought your pet fish for show-and-tell, but you really should have brought his fishbowl, too!"

6/84

"Cafeteria duty!"

6/85

"My music teacher is always comparing my ear for music with some artist. Who's Van Gogh?"

1/79

52

"Just think — a teacher goes to school and never gets out!"

"Rough day! We broke in a new teacher."

"What homework? These are hall passes, insurance forms, attendance reports, competency updates, and my grocery list."

"I've dedicated my life to mathematics. I've been teaching for $(9 + 3) \times 2 \div 4 \times 5$ years."

2/85

"Billy talks about you all the time. Most of us are getting pretty tired of hearing about you."

9/84

"Yes, your findings are correct. No, I don't believe you should publish your findings."

9/84

9/77

"Actually, this is not my real name, but it should keep any of you from calling me at home!"

4/85

"I would appreciate it very much if you wouldn't hum the theme from 'The Twilight Zone' every time I enter the classroom!"

12/83

"Try the experiment again, Renfrew. And remember — neatness counts."

2/69

"I used to teach nursery school. I taught this many years!"

10/84

"Yes, some adults paint like that, but we expect more from children."

1/85

"Wilson sometimes has a little difficulty handling parent conferences."

"Now, at the bottom of the page it says, 'Form into groups and discuss the first 12 stanzas.' What does T. S. Eliot mean by this?"

4/78

"I think there's been a misunderstanding. We advertised for someone to teach a canine curriculum, not a K-9 curriculum."

9/73

Financing Education

"So the Board of Education says we're on an austerity program. Now, I know it's going to be hard to put those grasshoppers back together again. . ."

1/74

"As you all know, funding responsibilities are shifting back to local governments."

9/83

"I showed my folks what I'm earning as a teacher. Now they're mad because I won't quit school and get a job."

9/73

"Mrs. Smith, there's been a change in our milk subsidy program."

10/77

"As a new college, we can't pay much, Coach, but we do have one fringe benefit — you don't have alumni to put up with."

"As you know, Miss Henson, the school board has had to stretch its resources rather thin. Could I have some of your lunch?"

11/83

"Sorry, kids, but this is the newest map we could afford."

"*Mr. Henshaw won't be here for the unit on the rise of unions in the 20th century. He's on strike.*"

"Byron needs $750 spending money to get through the second semester. He says that's only an educated guess."

5/84

"He knows all the answers, thank goodness! Saves us a bundle we'd have had to spend on a college education."

11/84

"Here's your outfit for the management team in the collective bargaining sessions."

11/83

"Since our children were too stupid for college, we have enough to live quite comfortably."

1/84

"You'll find 'School Budget Preparation Without Pain' under fiction."

11/83

Testing

"I have chosen a few last words — probably grammatically incorrect."

"We realize you do better on your IQ tests than you do in anything else, but you just cannot major in IQ."

"Jimmy tells me he's in the top 98% of his class. That sounds pretty good. . . . Hey, come back here!"

74

"I studied for this test, and the ploy paid off."

4/85

"I looked at the first essay question, and my whole life flashed before my eyes."

"We found a good nursery school. It's the only one where they start cramming for the SAT."

9/84

"A well-informed source, I'm not."

Controversial Subjects

"Why don't they compromise: allow prayer in public schools on test days only?"

5/85

"Observing a moment of silence sounds pretty good to me!"

3/85

"One way to make class more interesting would be to combine sex education with show and tell."

HEX
EDUCATION

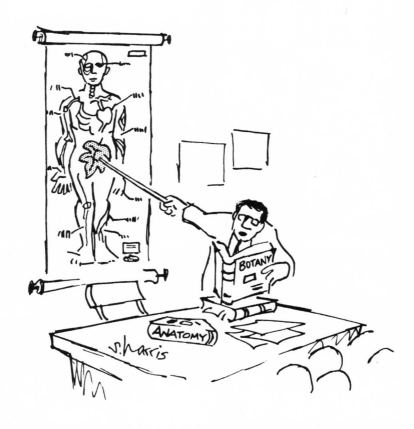

"Sex education classes sorta take the fun out of finding out about it on street corners."

6/84

"The good news is you're doing an excellent job and creating a great deal of interest in the sexuality class. The bad news is you're doing an excellent job and creating a great deal of interest in the sexuality class."

10/84

Discipline

"Kind of a tense day at school. We jangled Mrs. Reed's nerves early, and she hovered near the breaking point all day."

"Our fire drills present no problem in getting students out of the building. I'm open to suggestions on getting them back in."

3/79

"Mom, I'm allowed only one phone call, so. . ."

1/78

"Mr. Johnson certainly makes no attempt to make this any easier."

"Oh, dear! The students are flying poor Mr. Bugholtz again!"

"I'm not too clear on the difference between corporal and capital punishment."

9/84

"Now about our school's number-one problem: discipline. . ."

9/84

GRADE 6

"First, you have to get their attention."

1/84

"The rash has completely cleared up. You may redeploy him on the school system."

11/84

"I was sent home from school because my hair was too long and too short!"

"Come on. It's time to wage education."

1/85

"I didn't do it, honest."

3/85

2/85

"As a student teacher, the first thing you must learn is how to make your kids behave for you. My own successful disciplinary formula is based on understanding, firmness, determination, and all the bribery I can afford."

4/78

"It's great how Mr. Watson's able to communicate with kids on their own level!"

5/84

"My teacher wants a written excuse for my presence."

2/84

"On guard!"

9/84

"I'll tell you what's wrong with having a nonworking mother. She'll be there when I get home with this report card, that's what."

2/84

"And I think part of the problem is due to his short attention span."

2/84

STAND
IN THE
CORNER

9/84

"Actually, it's a rather old form of behavior modification therapy."

Graduation

"With all due respect for circumstance, I'd like to launch directly into extended pomp."

"Clayborn! This is indeed a surprise!"

6/84

"Dad, I've decided to change my major."

6/85

"Congratulations! You're free to go."

6/85

"The sound of the starter's gun will be the signal for each of you to come on stage and receive your diploma!"

6/84

"After considerable consultation with my colleagues, we have agreed that none of us has ever seen you before."

"For $32.50 I can have that framed for you."

"At least the gown won't show grease!"

6/84

"Due to a budget cutback, diplomas will be given out on a first-come, first-served basis."

6/85

"I hope those of you who turn out to be failures won't blame us."

1/84

"I don't think you understand, Steven! You're on your own now!"

6/84

"Frankly, I'll be glad to see you go!"

Finding Our Niche in Life

"I said to myself, 'Let life be thy teacher.'"

JAME'S
PRINTER'S

APOSTROPHE'S
OUR SPECIALTY

2/84

"That was my old high school teacher. He was checking to see if I had ever amounted to anything."

1/84

"When it comes to apathy, I just don't care."

"I would suggest that you get a good education, find a job that pays well, and be happy. I wish I could be more specific."

"Teacher said we had to make 'em."

THE BUCK FINALLY STOPPED HERE

3/79

MOTHER GOOSE
PUBLISHERS

CHILDREN'S CLASSICS

LUNCH TIME
12-1
NAP TIME
1-2

11/83

12/84

"I was your guidance counselor when you were a high school student here, Marvin, but now that you're on your own, you'll have to make your own business decisions."

2/84

E. HUBENHOWERINGHAMOWICZ
Ph.D.

BIG-NAME PROFESSOR

"I like your reading the financial pages, son. It shows you have an acquisitive mind."

9/85

"Because women in the workplace start out as girls in the classroom. That's why you have to go to school."

"We don't have lore. People in rural areas have lore. Here, you're on your own."

12/83

"There! Now can I become a lawyer?"

"No, this is the manuscript. That's the bibliography."

"This is from his early period."

"Buy low, sell high."

"Hey, Mac! Can't you read?"

10/84

"You're 18 years old, son. It's time for you to give up this idea of becoming a star basket-ball player and get on with your life."

3/85

The Cartoonists

GORDON BARTLETT

Born in Connecticut 67 years ago, he still lives there in spite of hating New England winters. He has been a newspaper office boy, commercial artist, soldier, door-to-door salesman, advertising salesman, advertising junior executive, laborer, and mental retardation supervisor, in that order. He likes cartooning because it is less tiring than any of these jobs.

GLENN BERNHARDT

"Some years ago I did a short bio for *Parade* magazine in which, trying for levity, I poked fun at my gardening ability by claiming to have developed a 'rose-less thornbush.' The editor, suspecting a slip on my part I suppose, changed that to a 'thorn-less rosebush' and for months I had to answer inquiries from astonished rose growers from all over. So this time I'll try to restrain myself and just give you the facts. . . ." Bernhardt admits he was born in St. Paul, Minnesota, and studied art at the Minneapolis Art Institute and then at the San Francisco Institute of Advertising Art. His interest in cartooning perked up when, on his first try, *Saturday Evening Post* bought two cartoons. His work has appeared in many anthologies, and he has published two books — *Cartoons/Bernhardt* and *How to Put Fun in Your Sex Life*. He and his wife Mary Lou live in Carmel, California.

DOUGLAS BLACKWELL

I was born on a warm summer day in 1954. Nothing very eventful occurred for another 26 years. Then I began cartooning. Since that time I've had cartoons published in over 100 magazines in the U.S. and Canada.

BO BROWN

Bo Brown has an A.B. degree from the University of Pennsylvania. He sold the first cartoon he submitted to *Saturday Evening Post* (then a nickel weekly of some repute) while attending law school at Penn. The dean granted him a leave of absence to give cartooning a whirl, and he's been whirling ever since.

FORD BUTTON

My 31 years as an art teacher gave me a backlog of humorous ideas that will extend into the 21st century. I hope that every teacher in this world will take time to laugh at my work. The nice thing about humor is you don't have to get a prescription for it.

MARTHA CAMPBELL

She was born and raised in Little Rock, Arkansas, where her first cartoons appeared in her high school newspaper. She graduated from Washington University, St. Louis, and was an artist for Hallmark. Now she lives in Harrison, Arkansas, with husband, 16-year-old daughter, and 11-year-old son.

THOMAS CHENEY

Tom Cheney was born in Norfolk, Virginia, and was raised in northern New York. After graduating from college with a B.A. in psychology and serving a short stint as a psychiatric counselor, he traded it all for a career in professional cartooning. Tom's work has appeared in over 200 national and foreign publications, among them: *New Yorker, Saturday Evening Post, Omni, National Lampoon, Saturday Review, Penthouse, Good Housekeeping, Cosmopolitan,* and *Woman's World*. He currently lives in Watertown, New York, with his wife and daughter.

OTHA COLLINS

Age: 45. Occupation: art teacher, Portsmouth Public Schools. For the past eight months or so, I have been working on my first book. It is a book about visual communication, targeted to educators.

For my volunteer efforts this past school year, I was awarded the 1985 Outstanding Service Award by the Portsmouth Education Association of the Virginia Education Association and the National Education Association.

I have also received an award for Distinguished Service from the Virginia Congress of Parents and Teachers, as well a life membership from the same organization.

FRANK COTHAM

My cartoons have appeared in such publications as *Wall Street Journal, Saturday Evening Post,* and *Punch* and have been published in several cartoon anthologies. I've also illustrated articles for *Reader's Digest*, the American Bar Association, and *Saturday Evening Post*. I work at home. My wife handles the business end, and my two children provide the background noise.

GLEN DINES

A resident of Fairfax, California (in elegant Marin County just north of elegant San Francisco), Glen Dines likes to think of himself as an elegant graphic satirist. The two ladies he lives with — lovely wife Rickie and a small, confused dog named Phred — will tell you differently.

Nevertheless, Glen is happy and tolerably well-fed. His cartoons have appeared in such diverse publications as *Quarter Horse of the Pacific Coast* and *Bulletin of the Atomic Scientists*.

JAMES ESTES

I am a native Texan, married to a native Texan, and we are proud parents of three native Texans. My wife Martha is a registered nurse. Son Robert is in his third year at West Point, daughter Kelley is a junior in high school, and daughter Paige is a fifth-grader. I have been cartooning for a little over 15 years. I enjoy family activities, reading, going to movies, long walks with Martha, and trading original cartoons with other cartoonists.

DAVE GERARD

Began cartooning career in 1935. Cartoons appeared in all national magazines, particularly *Saturday Evening Post* and *Colliers* during the '30s and through the '40s. Created a weekly feature titled "Viewpoint" for *Colliers* and a monthly feature titled "Will-Yum" for *Woman's Home Companion*. These appeared in 1947-1948 and 1949. Signed a contract to do daily/Sunday newspaper feature "Will-Yum." This feature appeared worldwide (eight languages) from 1949 to 1967. Then signed a contract with Register and Tribune Syndicate (now Cowles Syndicate) to produce a daily newspaper panel "Citizen Smith." This appeared in over 100 U.S. dailies from 1967 to December 29, 1984. Served two terms on Crawfordsville City Council, 1947 to 1955. Elected mayor of Crawfordsville on Republican ticket and served one term in that capacity 1972-1975. Received honorary doctor of humane letters degree from Wabash College, 1981.

Married Sarah Hunt in December 1934. Have two daughters and three grandchildren.

RANDY GLASBERGEN

Randy Glasbergen has been a full-time cartoonist since 1976. Approximately 7,000 of his cartoons have been published in *Good Housekeeping, Saturday Evening Post, Wall Street Journal, Woman*, and many, many others. His cartoons appear daily and Sunday in 200 newspapers and have been highly rated in reader surveys. Glasbergen also designs greeting cards for Hallmark and other companies and is frequently hired to do illustrations for advertising agencies, corporations, and publishers.

Glasbergen works at home with frequent interruptions from his wife, three daughters, two dogs, and four cats.

BOB HAGEMAN

I was born in Baldwin, Long Island, in the shadow of New York City, where, after graduating from art school and a sojourn as a technical illustrator, I embarked on a career as a freelance magazine cartoonist.

At the age of 47 with five or six thousand sales behind me, I moved to Florida where I've lived for the past five years and continue my cartooning via the mail along with some other art projects and a lot of swimming and where I'm considered "a young man in a hurry," which is the northern version of an "old fossil in a frenzy"!

RANDY HALL

Randy Hall owns an antique and coin shop in Liberal, Kansas, and enjoys drawing cartoons in his spare time. His work has appeared in most major publications including *National Enquirer, New Woman, American Legion*, and *Cosmopolitan*. Randy and his wife Marlene enjoy antiquing, fishing, and golf.

SIDNEY HARRIS

This year I should become pretty smart by osmosis, since my two children will be in college: Jennifer as a freshman, Jonathan as a senior. My most recent book, *Science Goes to the Dogs*, came about through the highest of motives: that is, backlash to all those confounded cat books. I now have my ear to the ground so that I can again get in on the end of the next trend.

JIM HULL

Jim Hull   2-26-43 - 6-0 -185-812-824-7657-317-44

-0866 - 740 4 - 47401 - 42 - 1 - Q - 62.

KYLE KASER

Born in Oregon in 1930. Attended the Portland Art Museum School and Portland State University. Taught art in secondary school for seven years. Currently working as the safety specialist for Portland Public Schools. Married 28 years to the same lady. Have a boy and a girl, both with BFA degrees. Cartooning has always been my first love, but until recently I have had little time to devote to it because of the need to earn a living and to help the kids get through college. My first cartoon sale was to the *Kappan*. Thanks.

EDWIN LEPPER

Born on August 6 or 7, 1913. Some doubt exists. Don't have a picture of myself, but the enclosed caricature does me justice. Self-taught as a cartoonist. After 35 years of gag cartooning, I'm still trying to figure out why editors usually buy my second-best cartoons.

TOM McCALLY

I am a slightly overweight (or undertall) English teacher with the Washington Local School system in Toledo, Ohio. I am 50 years old and have been married to the same lady 30 years. This entitles her to an endurance medal. We have three children and three grandchildren with a fourth on the way. I am an Air Force veteran. I taught four years in Toledo schools, then went to Washington. I have been teaching 22 years and someday hope to learn how to do it. I can truthfully say that at no time have I ever been mistaken for Paul Newman or asked to pitch for the Detroit Tigers — more's the pity.

BOB McCULLOUGH

Born and raised in Tennessee. Spent 12 years in the U.S. Navy, finally gaining enough courage to quit and pursue a life-long ambition of being an artist. I now reside on beautiful Lone Mountain in Morgan County with my wife and two children — and draw to my heart's content.

©1985 John W. H. Simpson

HENRY R. MARTIN

Henry Martin's cartoons have appeared in many national magazines and newspapers, including *ABA Press, American Scientist, Chicago Tribune, New Yorker, Saturday Review, Wall Street Journal*, and *Punch*. He has also published a number of cartoon collections, the most recent of which is *What's So Funny About Cartoons?* (Willis Kauffman, 1984).

JOEL PETT

Joel Pett is the editorial cartoonist for the *Lexington* (Ky.) *Herald-Leader*. His work has appeared in the *New York Times* and the *Washington Post*. A book of his cartoons, *Pett Peeves*, was published in 1982. Deadlines are the bane of his existence, and of the editors who work with him.

TONY SALTZMAN

Born Muskegon, Michigan, in 1938. Lived in Grand Rapids all his life. Started drawing cartoons as a gag, first sale to *Playboy*. Has appeared in over 300 publications: *Saturday Review, TV Guide, Playbill, Modern Bride*, and many specialized magazines. Two children.

CLEM SCALZITTI

Clem Scalzitti, 52 years old, a Scorpio, married, has four children and two grandchildren, has been a commercial artist since 1953. Self-employed for 19 years, he is now a graphic designer for Industrial Promotions, Inc. His work has appeared in *National Enquirer, Good Housekeeping, New Woman, New York Times*, and most of the male magazines. Now cartooning part-time and a VCR nut.

HARLEY SCHWADRON

Born in New York City, Harley Schwadron lives and works as a full-time cartoonist in Ann Arbor, Michigan. He has a newspaper background, working as an urban affairs writer for the late *Hartford* (Conn.) *Times*, a weekly newspaper editor, and an environmental writer and editor with University of Michigan Information Service. While working as a reporter, he began submitting his cartoons to magazines, and gradually his cartoon work began appearing with regularity in many national publications. In 1983 he received the Charles Schulz Award from United Feature Syndicate and the Scripps-Howard Foundation, honoring his work as a cartoonist. He has a B.A. degree from Bowdoin College in Maine, where he majored in philosophy, and a master's degree in journalism from the University of California at Berkeley. After college he was a Peace Corps volunteer in Thailand.

GODDARD SHERMAN

Rev. W. Goddard Sherman, Th.D., is a United Methodist minister, serving churches in Florida since 1953. A graduate of the Art Institute of Pittsburgh, he was a commercial artist at the time World War II began, at which time he was called into service and spent three years in the Solomon Islands. A graduate of Brown University and Pittsburgh Theological Seminary, Dr. Sherman served for several years on the faculty of the University of South Florida. During his ministerial career he has followed cartooning as a hobby, having work published by *Saturday Evening Post, Good Housekeeping, Changing Times*, and many others in addition to the *Phi Delta Kappan*. Now retired from the ministry, he makes his home in Valdosta, Georgia.

DUANE SIMSHAUSER

Married, three children (one still at home). My wife and I both teach sixth grade in a middle school in Ventura, California. I've been a sixth-grade teacher; high school arts/crafts teacher; junior high art/craft/ceramics teacher. Have been a part-time painter/sculptor after majoring in art and education at Eastern Washington State University. *Kappan* is almost exclusively my cartoon outlet, though the California Teachers Association and NEA have published a few. I get my ideas while jogging or cycling but am usually too tired and relaxed afterward to execute them. I'm 48 years old. Most of my work relates to bitter personal experience!

P. Steiner

PETER STEINER

Peter Steiner has been a cartoonist for six years. Before that, he was a professor of German at Dickinson College, Carlisle, Pennsylvania. His work has appeared in *New Yorker, Nation, Saturday Review*, and a number of other publications. He now does cartoons for the *Washington Times*.

TOM STRATTON

Tom Stratton is a cartoonist, writer, illustrator, stand-up comic, and humorist who has entertained audiences all over western New York. Nationally, he has performed his own particular brand of comedy in Las Vegas, San Francisco, Minneapolis-St. Paul, New York City, Los Angeles, Sarasota, and Buffalo. Of his appearances, Tom says, "I've learned not to perform in a tuxedo. The last time I was chloroformed, then woke up on top of somebody's wedding cake."

MICHAEL STREFF

This is a photograph of Michael Streff, age 36, about to eat a White Castle hamburger. He doesn't wear those glasses anymore and his hair is a little shorter, but you get the picture. (No pun intended.) His leisurely rise to success in cartooning has certainly astounded his old college friends, who are now rich graphic designers. He still has his own teeth and drives a 1962 Rambler with Volvo bucket seats.

BARDULF UELAND

I have been cartooning for some 30 years; an art instructor at the Agassiz Junior High School in Fargo, North Dakota, for 25 years; member of Phi Delta Kappa for 22 years; chairman of the Governor's Student Art Show in North Dakota (all-state, kindergarten through college) for 11 years; co-coordinator for the North Dakota section of "An Artistic Discovery" (U.S. House of Representatives art competition) for three years. And I am only 2̶1̶, 3̶1̶, 4̶1̶, or so years old!

RAY VOGLER

Ray Vogler is a research artist for General Motors Research Laboratories. He freelances for fun, and his work has appeared in 200 publications. He has a dog, a cat, and 20 goldfish.

JAN VAN WESSUM

Jan Van Wessum, who lives in an old wooden shoe in Amsterdam, gives cartooning the Dutch treat.

JOHN P. WOOD

John P. Wood is a 1985 graduate of the University of Minnesota and lives in Minneapolis. Currently, he is working in adolescent treatment at Golden Valley Health Center and looking for a teaching position in secondary social studies.